SØGAN UM TØLINI

THE NUMBER STORY

SMALL BOOK ONE

ENGLISH - FAROESE

Numbers Teach Children
Their Number Names

written and illustrated by

MISS ANNA

Early Reader Edition of *The Number Story 1*
Bronze Medal Winner, 2016 Wishing Shelf Book Award

Cover by | Lumpy Publishing
Layout by | Lumpy Publishing
Translated by Magnus Lamhuage
Coloring by Jieeun Woo and Maria Mirabella

Library of Congress Control Number: 2018902040

Names: Miss Anna, author.
Title: Number story : numbers teach children their number names / Miss Anna.
Description: Portland, OR: Lumpy Publishing, 2018.
Identifiers: ISBN 978-1-945977-81-7 | LCCN 2018902040
Summary: The pictures and rhymes present stories which introduce numbers 0-10.
Subjects: LCSH Numeration—English--Faroese--Pictorial works--Juvenile literature. | BISAC JUVENILE NONFICTION /
Languages: English--Faroese
Classification: LCC QA141.3 .M57 2018 | DDC 513—dc23

Publisher: Lumpy Publishing
Website: www.missannabooks.com
Email: missanna@missannabooks.com

Paperback: ISBN 978-1-945977-81-7
Printed in the U.S.A.   1 3 5 7 9 10 8 6 4 2

Vilt tú kenna okkara Tøl nøvn?

It is very easy and a lot of fun!

Tað er sera lætt og ordiliga stuttligt!

Say-along our little jingle

Syng við okkum hesa lítlu søgu!

starting from Number One!

Vit byrja við nummar eitt!

1

ONE looks like my one finger.

EITT

líkist mínum eina fingri.

ONE!
EITT!

2

TWO   trails a tail.

TYEY

hevur ein hala.

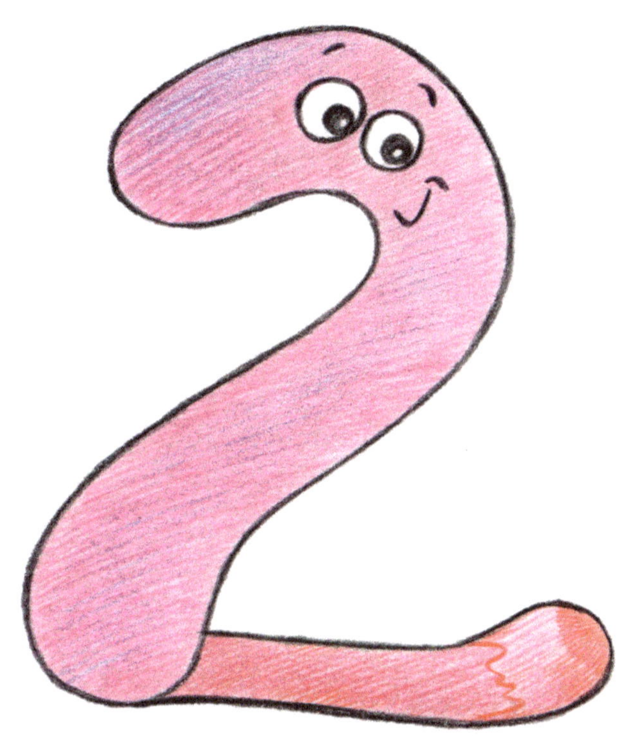

A TAIL! EIN HALI!

# 3

THREE   has bumps.

TRÝ

hevur buklur.

BUMPY! BUKLUT!

4

FOUR carries a sail.

FÝRA

hevur eitt segl.

Ein bátur við segli!

5

FIVE is a racing track.

FIMM

er ein rasarabani.

VROOM
VRUUUM!

6

SIX curves like a snail.

SEKS

bugar sum ein snigil.

A SNAIL! EIN SNIGIL!

7

S E V E N has a sharp angle.

SJEY

hevur eitt spískt horn.

BE CAREFUL! IT'S SHARP!
Ver varðin! Tað er spískt!

8

EIGHT is rollercoaster rails.

ÁTTA

er ein russjibani.

JUBII!
YIPPEE!

NINE is a bubble on a stick.

NÍGGJU

er ein bløðra á einum pinni.

A BUBBLE!   EIN BLØÐRA!

10

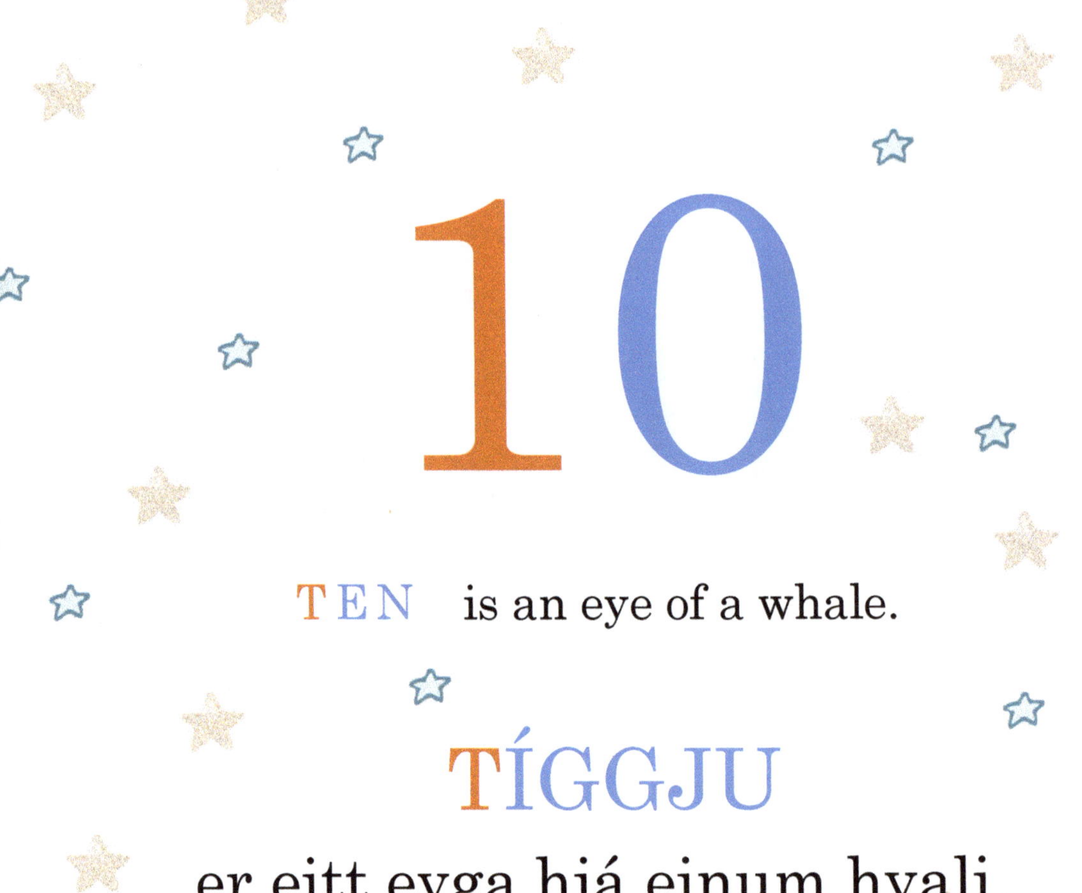

TEN is an eye of a whale.

TÍGGJU

er eitt eyga hjá einum hvali.

BLUNK!
WINK!
HELLO! HEY!

And

Og

O

ZERO   is an empty pail.

NULL

er ein tóm spann.

IT'S EMPTY!
Hon er tóm!

Thank you for playing with us today.

We had a lot of fun too!

Takk fyri at tú spældi við okkum í dag.

Vit høvdu tað eisini ordiliga stuttligt!

We are your Number friends,
Zero to Ten,
Who will be here for you~
Vit eru tínir tal vinir
Null til Tíggju.
Vit eru altíð beint við tína lið.

Bye-bye now!
See you again soon!
Bei-bei!
Síggjast aftur skjótt!

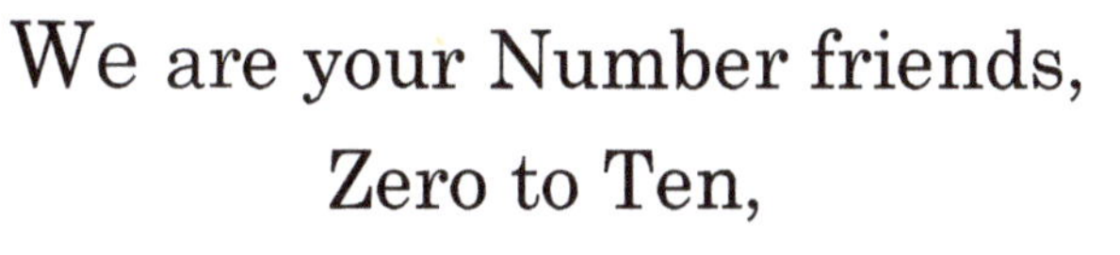

The Numbers are *SINGING* too!

To sing-a-long, look for Miss Anna Number Story
at your favorite music store like iTUNES.

MP3

Numbers 0-10
IDENTIFYING & COUNTING

Numbers 11-20
& Ordinals
first, second, third...

Numbers 0-100
& Place Values
ones, tens, hundreds...

About Clocks
& Telling Time
hours, minutes, seconds

Number Story 1 & 2
isbn: 978-0-996216-48-7

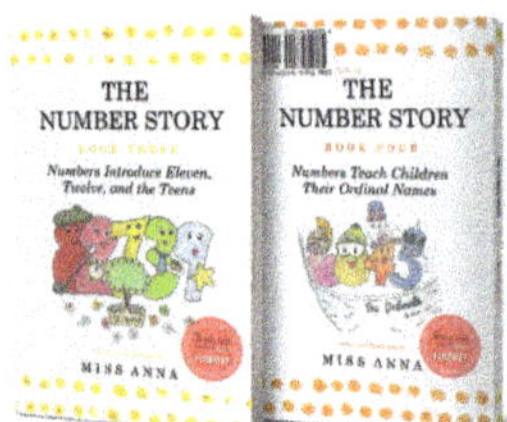

Number Story 3 & 4
isbn: 978-1-945977-01-5

Number Story 5 & 6
isbn: 978-1-945977-06-0

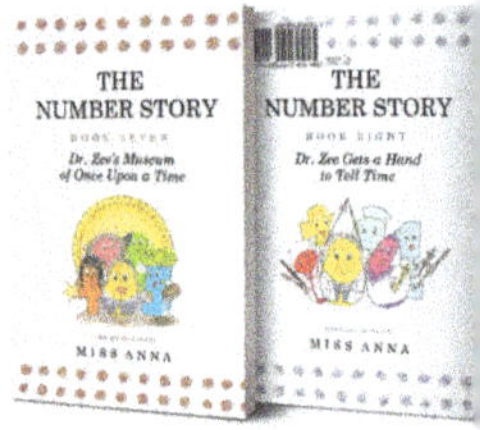

Number Story 7 & 8
isbn: 978-1-949320-40-

For more Miss Anna books to love,
visit us at

www.missannabooks.com

Numbers are working hard all over the world!
Come Travel the World with Us!